The Leading Salesman

Copyright © 2018, Stephen J. Blakesley and GMS Talent LP, all rights reserved.

No part of this publication may be reproduced or transmitted in any way without prior permission of the author except as provided by USA copyright law.

The Leading Salesman (cover)

Copyright © 2018, Stephen J. Blakesley and/or Taylor Roth, all rights reserved.

No part of this cover may be reproduced or transmitted in any way without prior permission of the author (Stephen J. Blakesley) or the cover designer (Taylor Roth).

Dedication

To my friend, partner and wife, Lillian.

Table of Contents

Forward ………………………………………………………………..4

Presence ………………………………………………………………..6

Motivation ……………………………………………………………10

Empathy ………………………………………………………………13

Communication ………………………………………………………16

Resilience …………………………………………………………….22

Emotional Intelligence ……………………………………………….25

Forward

The Leading Salesman

Everybody is selling something, so it is not unusual for people to focus on what makes them good or even excellent in that very effort. First, let me say that this book is not about managing salespeople (it seems that many want to be sales managers, but few strive to be salesmen). If you want information on managing salespeople, you would be more successful finding ways to do that somewhere else.

This book, *The Leading Salesman*, is about the attributes possessed by top salespeople, which also, to some degree or another, are found within each of us. To become a top salesperson, you will not only need to know these skills but be an expert in many of them.

The Leading Salesman is about the important attributes you will want to develop or leverage to distance yourself from competition. I do not intend to present all the attributes of top salespeople, just the ones I feel are fundamental and/or essential. You, of course, may have a different opinion, but that does not mean you are right or wrong, only different, and that is okay.

That claim being said, you may ask, *What makes you an expert?* My answer? *More than forty years of success in the roles of salesman and/or sales manager.* And many of those years were as the top salesman and then later, the top sales manager, but I would add, *Read the book, then tell me what you think.*

Throughout those years GMS Talent has, selected, and hired many salespeople narrowing down the essentials for excellence to just **six attributes.** In the coming pages I will share with you these six most important attributes that determine success as exemplified by exceptional performance. It is important to remember the designation "successful" because there are salespeople who are mediocre, in fact, there are more average salespeople than leading or successful ones. If you are an average salesperson, you may have achieved some success but not enough to consider yourself or have someone else consider you a top salesman.

The Leading Salesman is a book about the attributes of very good or exceptional salespeople, not just good or average salespeople. Growing the attributes that are identified here will lead to better and more sales, and if you continue to a successful sales career, these attributes will assist you in becoming better in a very difficult but most rewarding craft. This book is about a role that is among the highest-paid professions in the world and yet one of the most difficult ones to master. Most of us could use some help. If you improve in even one of these six attributes, you will see your stature and sales grow.

You will encounter many "rabbit trails" (not all leading to the rabbit) and obstructions that will frequently divert your efforts or maybe even convince you to pursue another course, but by first focusing on these six attributes, you can build a foundation of skills that will set you apart from others, not only in a sales role but in many other roles as well.

The six attributes are: **Presence, Motivation, Empathy, Communication, Resilience, and Emotional Intelligence**.

Chapter One

Presence

Whether you call it "presence" or something more common—like getting people to listen to you or just getting people's attention—is probably not too important. But, if you are hoping to lead, achieving exceptional success, being heard is of the greatest importance. If no one listens to you, your questions and claims will have little value. Thus, getting the attention of others is the beginning of the sales process. To become a successful and top salesperson, people must hear what you have to say.

Realizing that it is difficult to overcome a bad first impression, let's get ahead of the game and dive into the meaning of this mystical word. All top salespeople have presence. So, what is presence and how do you get it or create it?

In her book *Executive Presence*, Sylvia Ann Hewlett summarizes nearly two years of research on the topic of presence by suggesting that it consists of only three things:

>How you act (gravitas)
>
>How you speak (communication)
>
>How you look (appearance)

She suggests that these three attributes (gravitas, communication, and appearance) are universal. Although she does not say so specifically, establishing a presence is an essential task for any aspiring salesperson. Capturing the attention of potential buyers is job number one. If you do not have or get their attention, it is not likely you will make the sale.

If you don't give potential buyers a reason to listen to you, it is not likely you will capture their attention long enough to influence them, and influence is what sales is all about. People who have presence find it much easier to get the attention of others.

>Improving presence begins with measuring *gravitas*. "Gravitas" is an interesting word that few of us can clearly define. One of the best definitions I have heard in a long time

comes from Sylvia Ann Hewlett. She suggests that gravitas has six parts: confidence, decisiveness, integrity, emotional intelligence, reputation, and charisma.

On a scale of one to ten (with ten being the best), how would you rate yourself in these six parts? A score below forty would indicate that you have a need to improve in that area. A score below seven in any of these would warrant attention.

Evaluating yourself and the level you might reach in each of these parts is a good beginning but asking someone else to evaluate you is even better if you want to build your "gravitas."

Improvement in any of these six is easier said than done. To be sure, acting confidently requires a wide range of capabilities. The saying, "fake it until you make it" may apply. Controlling what we exude is a challenge. What others perceive of you is important. Do you display confidence? Is there a decisiveness about you? Are you a person with integrity (do you keep your word)? Do you understand how an event or happening has an impact on others? Do your deeds precede you? Do you have charisma (do you excite others)? Do you have clear goals? Are you dedicated to the achievement of the client's goals? These questions make up gravitas and have an impact on presence. Gravitas is, by far, the weightiest (at sixty-seven percent) of the three factors contributing to one's presence.

The second most important factor, in the creation of presence, is *communication* (twenty-eight percent). Are you a skilled communicator? What is it that identifies someone as a skilled communicator? Just understanding what makes one a good communicator is a good beginning. There are just three prevalent ways one communicates: by words, by body language, and by the inflection one gives to the words they speak.

Words. The size of your vocabulary sends a message about who you are. Many different research projects lend credibility to the thought that the greater your vocabulary, the more successful you will be. Of course, there are exceptions to everything, but improving your vocabulary will improve your image.

Inflection. Would you rather listen to Roseanne Barr or James Earl Jones? Speaking in an optimally appealing tone (125 Hz) has been found to be very important. The higher the pitch of your voice, the less you are heard. For instance, James Earl Jones speaks at about 85 Hz and Roseanne Barr at about 377 Hz. There has been much study on the pitch of one's voice and one's ability to earn big money. A 22 Hz drop in voice frequency correlates to an increase of $187,000 increase in annual earnings. WOW! The lesson here is that the lower the voice, the more the presence is enhanced.

And, finally, but most importantly, **body language** says more than anything else. It signals that you care and are paying attention and makes a big dent in your being heard. A good example is how distracting a cell phone is and how detrimental it can be to one's image. Paying attention to your cell phone when other things are happening is certainly a no-no. It is so disrespectful for someone to be texting or reading a message while someone else is talking or presenting. Body language is a way of showing respect. For instance, gaining eye contact, leaning toward the speaker, and giving signals that you are really listening like nodding your head in agreement. Learning to use body language as a tool to enhance your presence is a valuable skill.

So, to add value to your communication skills and increase your presence, you might consider reading *How to Win Friends and Influence People* by Dale Carnegie or *Ask More* by Frank Sesno. You may want to analyze your voice and make the necessary adjustment or pay less attention to your cell phone.

The third and final aspect of presence is *appearance* (five percent). There are just two important points here, and one has to do with your physical appearance. Here is an example of what I mean: Once, I was on a plane, and the gentleman across the aisle from me was amazingly distracting. The hair in his ears had grown to such a state that he looked like one of those Chia Pets that has grass growing in all directions. The hair in his ears or, I should say, out of his ears was such that I was amazed he could hear at all. I would not follow that guy.

Another example is bad teeth. Teeth, especially bad ones, can sometimes be more distracting than what a person is saying. So, paying attention to how you look is a key piece to creating the presence you wish to exhibit.

One of the most valuable things my mother gave to me was a sense of color matching. She was a real teacher when it came to the certainty of matching colors and what clothes to wear for which occasion. Admittedly, appearance is a smaller percent of presence, but sometimes little things mean a lot. Cut the hair in your ears and nose, fix your teeth, if needed, and make certain you reflect the image you wish to present.

It is important to understand that presence does not come with the title of salesman but rather as a precursor to the title. It is true that some think that being a salesman is easy and not very glamorous. So just when does presence become a requirement? Some believe that you first obtain the position and then develop presence, but it should be the opposite: exhibit the presence and you will get the listening and attention you deserve.

Nothing will cause a "short circuit" in your sales efforts quicker than poor appearance.

T- shirts and tennis shoes are just not proper. Get attention by dressing exceptionally.

Chapter Two

Motivation

Are you motivated? That is a simple enough question, right? "It is too broad," you might say. "Motivated to do what?" would be a legitimate follow-up question. Are you motivated to understand what motivates you and everything around you?

Do you know what motivates you? Is your motivation consistent with someone who is successful in sales? I would suggest that you survey some of the top salespeople you know. Don't base the decisions you make about the top salespeople on whether you like that person or not, but on whether they are truly the top salesperson in the organization or at least among the top. Ask them, "What motivates you to be a top salesperson?"

Psychologically speaking, people behave as they do because their values (or what is most important to them) push them in that direction. People are motivated by their values. If their values do not get satisfied, they become unhappy, and unhappy people are seldom top performers. So, if we want to know why a person behaves the way they do, like turning in the top sales numbers month in and month out, understand what they value most. For example, if someone values their family more than anything else, it is safe to say that they believe that providing for that family is very important.

Providing for a family is costly and requires a lot of hard work, like arriving on time, working until the job gets done, and other efforts that many are not willing to make. You might translate those efforts into a utilitarian motivation (money, efficiency, return on investment) and the things that it can bring: working hard equals making more money. Simplistic? Yes, but also realistic. Is there anything else?

Yes, in addition to realizing that money is important, being able to CONTROL the amount of money is equally so. Having the desire to apply yourself (your skills) and control the amount of money you will earn is an important trait of successful salespeople. In fact, being in control of the amount of money one makes is one of the foundations on which great salespeople build.

Self-esteem, however, is often the number one factor contributing to self-motivation. How you feel about your self determines exactly how and to what level you can motivate yourself. Salespeople need a lot of self-esteem.

I would say that self-esteem stands tall among those factors that contribute to sales achievements. With a low self-esteem, one would have a difficult time making a living in a sales role. What exactly is self-esteem?

It begins with the acceptance of ourselves—how we value ourselves. If we think of ourselves as lowly, incompetent, incapable individuals, we will not likely take on additional or more difficult tasks, but instead find ourselves satisfied to hover around the lowest level of achievement. On the other hand, if we think of ourselves with capabilities and talents at a higher level believing that we are important and matter to ourselves and others, we are much more likely to target achievements at a higher level.

But that is not all. A person with high self-esteem has an optimistic view about where they are going and whether they are willing to accept the responsibility for the outcome of their efforts. Also, one must understand and accept the differing opinions of others. Being willing to accept the blame but being resilient enough to bounce back and start again if things don't work out like you expected is an indicator of high levels of self-esteem.

It is true that emotions play a big part in motivation and self-esteem. You are not likely to be a highly motivated individual without a high level of self-esteem.

Hendrie Weisinger, Ph.D., in his book *Emotional Intelligence at Work*, speaks of four sources of self-motivation: Yourself, Supportive Friends, Emotional Mentor, and Your Environment. Of these four, let's focus on "Yourself."

Looking to yourself for motivation is challenging at times. So a little help can't be all bad. Optimism is a good place to begin because it is the anchor for high performance in a salesperson. It is the beginning of a *positive attitude.* Being optimistic depends a lot on self-talk. We talk to ourselves a lot, but we often don't say the right words.

It is so important that we learn to say the right things: *I can make this sale* or *It will be easy to contrast the reasons to buy my widget versus some other* or *I can easily overcome any objections*. Write these statements down on 3 x 5 cards. Review them before you go on your next sales appointment. You may feel somewhat awkward at first, but what you have written down will surface and be easily expressed in a real-time experience.

Chapter Three

Empathy

Empathy requires two of the four foundation skills - (Self-Awareness, Self-Management, Social Awareness, and Social Management) used to measure Emotional Intelligence: Social Awareness and Social Management. The question then becomes, *How do we become more aware of others, and how do we better manage the emotions of others?*

Having empathy is certainly a learned skill. Since it involves others, it may be easier for us to focus on those things that have a positive impact (we typically seem to have greater difficulty focusing on ourselves than we do focusing on others). To sell or influence a buying decision, a great sales talent must be able to understand how those to whom they are selling feel. A skillful salesperson will put themselves in the buyer's shoes (something easier said than done) to understand how the other person feels.

Just as a practice exercise, when meeting a new prospect, ask yourself these questions:

Are they comfortable and at ease?

Are they looking for answers, or do they already have their minds made up?

Are they insecure about getting value?

Do they understand my role?

What is my role?

Do they trust me?

Do my questions seem sincere?

In other words, attempt to determine the prospect's wants and needs. Address those needs before you try to sell or influence them into buying anything. In most cases, time spent understanding your prospect gives them a sense that you care about them (and hopefully you do).

When placed in a buying situation, the prospect has three options: they can buy from you, they can buy from your competition, or they do not buy at all. What your competition is doing is an important piece to the sales puzzle. The best salespeople know what the competition has and is doing. Do you? See how well you know your competition.

Answer these questions:

Who is my competition?

What do they have that I don't have?

Do they have a better price?

Do they have better quality?

Is their customer service better?

Do I have stories that help prospects see a difference?

Of course, if you do not have answers to these questions then your next action is obvious—get them! If you do have answers and they favor the competition, those will likely be obstacles, and you will have to overcome them. The point is, BE PREPARED. Don't just "shoot from the hip." You need good, credible answers when the competition is mentioned. Know your competition.

Have a plan. A simple model to making a sale is to follow a plan. It is a good idea to have several exploratory questions that will give you insight into and help you understand the prospect. "Why" questions are always good for providing insight into the prospect's wants and needs. For example, *Why is quality so important to you?* or *Why is price so important to you?* And it is always good to dig a little deeper with at least one more question like *How does quality affect your decision?*

Your questions say to the prospect, *Hey, this person is listening to what I am saying and wants to get greater clarity. They listen to me and realize that my concerns are only my concerns, but they are very important to me.* This effort in building your understanding of the prospect is the first part of empathy. I just recently got off the phone with my daughter, Nancy, who is a top salesperson in the insurance industry. I asked her, "What is the single most important thing that makes you so good at sales?" She said, "Relationships. If you build a relationship with someone, they will remember you forever." Being aware of those around us is the first step toward social management, the second part of empathy.

Influencing others is at least in part dependent upon our ability to understand a situation. Understanding the situation and doing something about it is emotional intelligence. Developing the ability to manage an environment that includes ourselves and others is a unique ability. A buying situation is a social management opportunity. You can orchestrate atmosphere no matter where you are. Here is one example of the management of a social environment with which we are all familiar.

My wife, partner, most loved, now with Jesus, was alerted that our son-in-law had, in a heated argument with his spouse (our daughter), hit her. When this event was reported to my wife, she immediately got in the car and drove several miles to manage the situation. Our son-in-law was doing some tractor work for a friend, and my wife drove to his location with a baseball bat, stopped the car where he could see it, and waited for him to come to her, which he did. She delivered this message, baseball bat in hand: *If you ever hit my girl again, I will come after you with this bat*. He never touched our daughter again! Now that was managing the environment and the individual simultaneously! Very emotionally intelligent!

Empathy, then is more than just seeing things through other's eyes and/feeling how others feel, it involves action. Doing something to bring about change. Empathy is about seeing things as others see them, understanding how the other person feels, but acting to demonstrate what you have sensed.

Chapter Four

Communication

Communication is so important it has its own chapter. Being a critical part of one's presence (Gravitas, Communication and Appearance), we talked about it in Chapter One, Now I want to expand on its value. Apart from the importance communication has in establishing presence, it plays a key role in making the sale. One of the best examples of salesmanship, was demonstrated nearly a quarter century ago by Franklin Delano Roosevelt (FDR). During the early years of his first term, he sold his idea for another agency to his cabinet. An idea he believed would impact the attitude of our country and but it on track to recovery. The idea was the *Civilian Conservation Corps (*CCC*)*.

The CCC was the brainchild of Franklin, himself and it proposed a method of putting 250,000 young men (18-25) to work and gave them hope during the depression years (1929-1939). The forests of this great country, it seems, had fallen into disarray during those years, due to lack of funds. The concept of the CCC would not only renew the forest lands, but give hope and meaning to the lives of a new generation. One that would be responsible for the future. Doris Kearns Goodwin, in her book *Leadership*, wrote "the CCC would heal the forest while healing the young men." (I like that thought)

The idea of the CCC was, to put 250,000 young men to work, doing something that would not only heal them but help heal the country, a country that had struggled yet deteriorated during the depression. It would give this new generation something constructive to do and help provide for their families, back home, since a portion of their pay would be sent directly to them.

Selling the idea of a new agency to his cabinet was considered a "pipedream," by its members. They had many questions, good ones and pertinent ones, like, how would you recruit this many young men and transport them around or who would supervise these young people? The cabinet first considered the idea hastily thought up and drawn up. For instance, the program was to be up and running in only 3 months. How could this happen, asked the cabinet members?

It did happen and the reason it did was Roosevelt's salesmanship. He proposed such a clear picture of how it could be done with conventional resources that the cabinet could hardly refuse. They adopted the plan because Roosevelt used the basic principals of salesmanship – **clearly defining the problem, outlining the obstacles that might be encountered, providing a reasonable solution and finally implementing the plan.** The idea of the CCC was very difficult to turn down because it proposed a positive step that would address the problem and make a difference. Roosevelt, if nothing else, was a communicator.

Communication is more than just talking, however. Most of us are so focused on talking that we sometimes forget about the most important part of communication—listening.

In almost every survey GMS Talent LP has taken over many years in the training industry, listening comes in at the top or close to the top when asked, "What is the most important communication factor?" Yet listening is always the most underdeveloped part of communication. Someone once said communication is more than just waiting to talk. Communication is a two-way street: it needs both the physical transference of information by (in this case) voice and listening to what a prospect or another person has to say.

Let's investigate listening. First, let me say that I am not the world's best listener. I am working on becoming a better listener, but I am not where I want to be yet. Here is an example of just how terrible I used to be. I was in downtown Dallas for the Texas–Oklahoma Cotton Bowl, and the whole downtown area was really buzzing. I was at my hotel, and I wanted to go to the game. However, I was not familiar with Dallas, and I needed directions. I asked a couple in the hotel lobby, but they did not know. I am not a good listener, but I am a good reader of people, and these two were honestly trying to be helpful, but I sensed they did not really know for sure how to get to the Cotton Bowl, and since I had limited time and did not want to get lost, I filtered out what they had to say. I kept looking for someone I could trust to give accurate information. Finally I saw a policeman and felt that he would know how to get there. He was busy supervising something, and I was reluctant to interrupt, so I waited until he finished what he was doing or was at least at a place where he could be asked a legitimate question and give me a usable answer, considering I was totally unfamiliar with the city. I asked the simple question, "How do I get to the Cotton Bowl from here?" Guess what? He had a believable answer, but being the poor listener that I am, I listened to the whole string of directions but "heard" only the first half of those directions. I was too embarrassed to ask him to repeat himself, so I thanked him, hopped into my rental car, and went as far as my memory of his directions would take me. I then had to stop and find another reliable source to get me to my final destination. So, you can see why I want to get better at listening, and this example is a good one of common listening failures (not hearing well).

Certainly, we could all become better at listening. Mark Goulston, in his book *Just Listen*, suggests that we filter what we listen to and ultimately hear what we want. Certainly, I filtered the information I received, but he suggests that we usually filter things, sometimes more than others, using these familiar filters:

- Gender
- Generation
- Nationality
- Education
- Emotion

Sometimes we don't really listen because we have already decided that what we are hearing is inaccurate, or not worth considering. Maybe "not worth considering" is a salesperson's Achilles' heel when it comes to listening. Too many salespersons are just too smart to succeed. They misperceive too much, assume too much, and think they know too much. Here is a listening checklist that might help:

1. Remember that you and the potential buyer would not likely be together if the buyer did not perceive that you or what you were selling could help them— **Respect, Respect, Respect** (it is not about you).

2. Gather as much information as you can (ask questions) about <u>their</u> needs.
3. Make certain you understand their "real" need (ask more questions).
4. Ascertain that their wants might be appropriate as well (ask more questions).

We have all experienced salespeople who talk too much. Maybe we have even reached a place where we are saying to ourselves, "I wish this guy would shut up, so I can make up my mind." Please take note. Rambling and talking more than is necessary is a sign of inexperience and/or disrespect, and we do have a natural tendency to give people too much information.

A good example of providing too much information comes from a mentor of mine, Jim Rohn. He tells the story of the car salesman who gives the prospective buyer more information than they want and loses the sale. The encounter goes something like this: *The salesman and the prospect meet on the showroom floor. The prospect has come to buy a car, knows the make and model they want, but seeks a little additional information. The salesman wants to make certain he gives the prospect every piece of information he thinks they need but does not ask them what they want to know. Instead, he suggests that the prospect meet him in the garage where he begins to tell them everything there is in the guidebook in the glove compartment. Well, that is more information than the prospect wants. As a result, the client gets bored and walks away (still as a prospect but not as a prospect for this salesman).* People don't really need a lot of information, they just need the right information. But how do you know the right information? Use a novel approach—ask them!

Keep in mind that the goal is to meet the prospect's needs and wants. If you are a salesperson, it is a good thing to have certain questions ready in order to gather enough information to match your product or service with the client's needs and wants. But don't overdo it! Please remember that you are supposed to be the expert in matching the product with the desires of the client.

The ability to ask questions is not difficult, but asking the right ones is the real challenge. Asking the right questions depends a lot on preparation. Remember, when you get to the point of asking questions, you are at work. So rule number one is to be brief, sincere, and friendly, and most importantly, self-confident. How much preparation will you do? You (the salesperson) should be talking twenty percent of the time and listening eighty percent. To do that requires skill and advanced planning.

If you want the prospect to talk eighty percent of your time together, you should not wait until you meet to think of meaningful questions (if you do not prepare ahead of time, you will not likely be able to reach the goal of eighty percent). There are several different types of questions that can be prepared in advance: warm-up questions, get-acquainted questions, discovery questions, and wrap-up questions. Here are a few examples:

Warm-up questions:

Help me to get to know you better. What is most important to you?

What pushed you here today?

Get-acquainted questions:

What is compelling you to investigate purchases, today?

Give me a little background on your family?

Discovery questions:

What is it that is making you think you need a new/different widget?

Would you rather buy less expensive or more productive?

Wrap-up questions:

Were you planning to buy today or soon?

What else do you need before you can decide?

Of course, you can likely come up with even better questions, but these should get you to a place of focus. Just remember, the more you know about your prospect, the higher the likelihood you will make the sales.

Then last, but certainly not least, is the way you say something. Salespeople, for the most part, need to be great communicators. Certainly, how you say something has a major impact on how and when the prospect will hear you.

Deborah Tannen in her article "Who Gets Heard and Why" says it right when she says *it is not as simple as saying what you mean*. But real communication goes even farther. everything you say should be said in a certain way. Great salespeople are skillful at saying things the right way. She offers some thoughts on how messages are delivered and heard. We add our opinion on the value it brings to the sales process.

Style of Talking	Unintended Consequences	Sales Use
Sharing Credit-*frequently*	*Speaker does not get credit*	*Admiration for giving*

uses "we" instead of "I" in speaking	for accomplishments	credit to others!
Asking Questions-asks questions to gather knowledge	Speaker appears stupid	Helps to grow knowledge of prospect's wants and needs
Giving Feedback-noting weakness only after stating strengths	Confusion about what is important	Showing that you care and have listened enough to be able to consider improvement

These are only a few of the examples of unintended conclusions reached and how they might be used to further influence the prospect.

Chapter Five

Resilience

Resilience is about the ability to get up and start again or the ability to bounce back after you encounter difficulty. And as a salesperson, you will certainly encounter many roadblocks and obstacles. A "fancy" definition of resilience might be something like this: *The process of adapting well in the face of adversity, trauma, tragedy, and threats. The ability to recover from almost anything.* That is the way I look at resilience. In a sales role, having or developing the ability to recover from rejection is something you will need to do most frequently. Some of us have a greater level of resilience than others because we worked on developing it, or we were born with a somewhat higher level of resilience and then added to it. Having resilience and using it are essential if you are to distance yourself from your competition. The absence of resilience can "kill" or "depress" the other five skills in your Sales Success Skill Set (*The Leading Salesman*).

No, No, No, and H*## no! These are dreaded words no salesperson wishes to hear. Sometimes success seems far away. What then does a salesperson do when the prospect says NO? The best advice I can give is to continue to look for the objection and be persistent in asking for agreement and ultimately the sale. The good thing about resilience is that it is a skill and can be learned. Here are just a few strategies to build up or strengthen your resilience:

#1. Prepare in advance! Expect a "no." Answer this question: *What will I do if the prospect says no?* Many will just fold or quit and never darken the selling door again, but the superior performer will seek a way to overcome the no. Expect the "no" and devise a simple way around it. A simple but effective question is, *What is it that is keeping you from committing?* Just remember, getting the "yes" sometimes begins with a "no."

#2. Define the win! Know what you want to achieve going into the experience. Answer the question, *What do I hope to get from this encounter?* Define the win. To win is to make the sale. Often to make the sale you must move through that dark and scary place of rejection. No one likes to be rejected, but if you know that the rejection brings you closer to the win then you can be encouraged. Here are a couple of attitude requirements:

#1. Internal motivation! Find a means of motivating yourself to overcome rejection. Often, reading and internalizing the way others have achieved victory over rejection is helpful. Your motivation and your self-talk is, possibly, one of the most important attributes contributing to making the sale.

#2. Never give up! Be like the Energizer bunny—just keep on going no matter what. Find a means of overcoming. Take direction from Winston Churchill whose graduation speech to youngsters graduating from the same high school as he consisted of only three words: "Never Give Up!"

Bouncing back is easier for some than others. The environment in which we live and work does affect our ability to bounce back. Our environment is important to many aspects of our lives. Those with financial security, a good education, a challenging career, etc. are more likely to have an easier time bouncing back than those who have a challenging financial position, a poor education, and/or a boring job. And as such, each of us has a choice.

We do spend a lot of time on the importance of parents and managers creating an environment where people can be the best they can be. If you find yourself in a hole and unable to get out, evaluate the environment in which you live and work. If needed, take steps to improve it.

Steven M. Southwick, M.D. and Dennis S. Charney, M.D. co-authored the book *Resilience–The Science of Mastering Life's Greatest Challenges*. They wrote about resilience factors such as Fear, Realistic Optimism, Cognitive and Emotional Flexibility, and several others. They say "a person's level of resilience will determine who succeeds and who fails." I agree. A salesperson is knocked down more than others. Factually, it requires a lot of energy to recover from a setback (a "no!"). A person must be skillful and mastering the mind. If there is no awareness, the mind will take you down many rabbit trails and push you right into an obstruction that may hold you back for a lengthy period, or sometimes for forever.

But what is said about resilience and having resilience is true. If you cannot recover from even a small setback, like a "no," how can you move ahead?

Chapter Six

Emotional Intelligence

Emotional intelligence (EI) is an essential sales requirement that makes the other five skills better. Having EI increases your likelihood of success in a sales role by a considerable amount. I teach EI to domestic and foreign executives. It is a fun course to teach but requires a real commitment to the understanding and controlling of the emotions we deal with every single day.

Even the first step—identifying the emotion with which we may be dealing—is sometimes challenging, to say the least. Over the years I have asked the question, "Why do we work so hard at understanding and fixing others when we are so inadequate in understanding and fixing ourselves?"

To keep it simple, let's begin with the *Four Quadrant Model* of Emotional Intelligence: Self-Awareness, Self-Management, Social Awareness, and Social Management. Number one on our list is always Self-Awareness (we all need to be self-aware). I recently read that most people believe they are self-aware, but they really are not. That belief holds true in our personal work. Most of us just do not know much about ourselves. So, a few exercises focused on what is most important to someone (their values) and why they do what they do (their purpose) is always enlightening and exciting.

Here is an exercise to help you evaluate where you might be regarding Self-Awareness. Answer these five questions and evaluate your answers:

1. *How do I feel about myself?*
2. *How do I believe others see me?*
3. *What are the five most important things in life to me?*
4. *Where am I going in life?*
5. *What is my purpose in life?*

If you are satisfied with your answers, go on to the next step: Self-Management.

We frequently do not have control over our emotions, but those who do are much more emotionally capable than those who don't. For instance: someone says something with which you don't agree. Often there is an emotional experience there. The emotion could be anger, or it could be just about anything. An example occurred just a few days ago: I was coming home from church with my daughter and we decided to get some Chinese food before she left for home. I pulled into a Chinese place I frequent and on the door in big black letters was a sign that said, "Open Xmas and New Year." I might have become angry and maybe not even entered the place. Instead, we entered and greeted the guy who seated us, but not without saying that the word was Christmas, not Xmas. He apparently did not speak English very well and only smiled and nodded before he sat us. In the past, I might have gotten angry, but instead I thought that there might be a more successful way to approach the issue. So, as we were leaving, I stopped and spoke to the two gentlemen in the next booth and pointed out the problem (they did not know exactly what to do or say). I went on to the next booth and pointed out that it was Christmas, not Xmas, and got a thumbs up from that couple. I asked that they mention the error on leaving. I don't know whether they did, but I did manage my emotions and maybe made a stronger point (or at least one that would be thought about after I left). I did manage my "anger" emotion there and hopefully made some forward progress (I will have to return before Christmas and see if they took the sign down or see if there were any changes).

Those kinds of opportunities present themselves frequently. They also make the point that "you catch a lot more flies with honey that you do with vinegar" (my grandmother taught me that). Whether it is letting others know you don't accept "Xmas" as a substitute for Christmas or some other event that creates an emotion, being able to recognize the emotion, pause and handle it in a manner that will get the results you desire rather than deepening the issue is emotional intelligence.

Here are five steps you should consider as tools for emotional management:

1. Use a journal for a short period to help you identify the emotions you experience during a work day. When you experience an emotion, take a moment and write down that emotion in your journal.
2. Next, try to think back to determine what "triggered" the emotion.
3. Understand that you are sensitive to the triggers and learn to manage them.
4. Learn to use the "pause" for two things: think about the emotion and what caused it, and think about what has been said or done.
5. Always focus on the outcome. Is it what you wanted or something else? Remember the universal formula for lifetime success (E + R = O), where E represents the events that come into our lives (largely without control), R represents our response to those events and O is the outcome that we desire. In other words, we control the outcome of most any event by our response. We are (actually) in control. We control the outcome by our response.

The next piece of EI is Social Awareness. Social Awareness is simplified to an awareness of the environment. Here are five questions you can ask that will quickly sum up the environment and create Social Awareness:

1. What kind of people are around me?
2. What are they saying?
3. How does what they are saying make me feel?
4. What are these people doing to me?
5. Is all of that okay?

The final piece to becoming Emotionally Intelligent is Social Management. Learning to manage the people and the space that influences the way you feel is social management. Here are five questions you will want to consider:

1. How can I manage the physical environment?
2. Have I asked enough questions?
3. Do I have a clear picture of my prospect's needs and wants?
4. Am I able to overcome any negative impact place and space may have?
5. Can I manage the environment in a positive manner?

One Final Suggestion!

Ask for the money!

Bibliography

Goleman, Daniel. *Emotional Intelligence*. New York: Bantam, 1997.

Goleman, Daniel. *Social Intelligence*. New York: Bantam, 2006.

Goulston, Mark. *Just Listen*. New York, AMACOM 2010.

Hewlett, Sylvia Ann. *Executive Presence*. New York: Harper-Collins, 2014.

Pink, Daniel H. *To Sell is Human*. New York: Penguin, 2012.

Southwick, Steven, M.D., and Dennis Charney, M.D. *Resilience—The Science of Mastering Life's Greatest Challenges*. New York: Cambridge University Press, 2012.

Stein, Steven J., Ph.D. *Make Your Workplace Great*. Mississauga, Ontario, Canada: Wiley and Sons, 2007.

Tannen, Deborah. "The Power of Talk: Who Gets Heard and Why." *Harvard University Review Press*.

Weisinger, Hendrie, Ph.D. *Emotional Intelligence at Work*. San Francisco: Jossey-Bass, 2000.

www.ingramcontent.com/pod-product-compliance
Lightning Source LLC
Chambersburg PA
CBHW081624220526
45468CB00010B/3017